THE SEARCH CONTINUES

The Journey

KEVIN DOWNSWELL

minna
PRESS
www.minnapress.com

Scripture quotations are taken from The Holy Bible, King James Version. Cambridge Edition: 1769; King James Bible Online, 2014. www.kingjamesbibleonline.org
and The Holy Bible, New Living Translation, copyright ©1996, 2004, 2007 by Tyndale House Foundation. Used by permission of Tyndale House Publishers, Inc., Carol Stream, Illinois 60188. All rights reserved.

National Library of Jamaica Cataloguing-In-Publication (CIP) Data
Downswell, Kevin

    The search continues : the journey / Kevin Downswell.

    p. ; cm.

ISBN 978-976-95693-5-5 (pbk)

1. Downswell, Kevin   2. Gospel musicians – Jamaica
3. Biography   I. Title

920   dc 223

Executive Editor: Lena J. Rose
Book Layout: Mark Steven Weinberger
Cover Images: William Richards

Published in Kingston Jamaica by Minna Press
www.minnapress.com

Ordering Information
Quantity (Bulk) Sales: Special discounts are available on quantity purchases by corporations, associations, and others. For details, contact the publisher: sales@minnapress.com

KEVIN DOWNSWELL
MINISTRIES
www.kevindownswell.com

www.facebook.com/kevindownswellministry
www.twitter.com/kevindownswell
www.instagram.com/kevindownswell
www.myspace.com/kevindownswell

Dedication

This book is dedicated firstly to my darling wife Marsha, who if not for her patient and loving encouragement, I would not be where I am today.

To my mother Miriam, who inspires me in so many ways.

To my team which includes Wendell Lawrence and Spurr Music Empire, my band and my singers, for being my hands and feet, and my engine that keeps me moving forward.

I also dedicate this book to all my supporters and to those who refuse to settle for less than God's best for them. Also, to those who refuse to fold their hands and lie down, but instead press forward against all odds simply because, like Peter in the boat, God's voice says "come". May you find grace and strength to walk where His voice leads.

Table of Contents

Foreword

The greatest gift to humanity occurred around 2000 years ago. "For God so loved the world that he gave his only begotten son" (John 3:16). Around the fourth millennium B.C.E., there was a gift of not equal but, nevertheless, incalculable value.

The gift of writing.

Starting with the Sumerians, spreading through Egypt and the Middle East; later to Greece, China, India and the Americas, humankind developed the art of expressing knowledge, ideas, feelings, occurrences and the like; first utilizing pictographic then ideographic and later (about the fourteenth century B.C.E) alphabetic writing systems. The Greek response to writing was extraordinary, with books on philosophy, law, poetry and drama pouring out around 500 B.C.E. The production of books got a big boost with the invention of paper by the Chinese between 100 B.C.E. and 105 B.C.E. and block printing of texts by the sixth century.

Regrettably, Jamaicans have not made sufficient use of this communication medium. Due to Jamaica's high rate of illiteracy and a general disinterest in reading, it is often jokingly said: If you want to keep something important hidden from Jamaicans put it in a book, This fact has discouraged many would-be authors.

Kevin Downswell is deserving of the highest commendation for his vision, perseverance and courage in producing this book. It is rare that one who puts words to harmony also writes words to produce a book. When that individual is a Jamaican, that's not only rare but a special occurrence.

There is something else that's special about Kevin Downswell and his book. When his harmony and words are combined to make music, the words (lyrics) are what ministers to the soul; and they do so in a way that goes beyond the soothing effect experienced by Saul when David played on his harp. The scripture declares in Romans 10:17 that "faith cometh by hearing and hearing by the word of God". Some music is instrumental. I will avoid a debate about whether one can be truly saved by just the playing of instruments.

In my mentoring of Kevin Downswell, I have been consistent in saying to him, "you are a minister who sings; not a singer who ministers". The ability to sing melodiously combined with a riveting stage presence, manifest themselves with each Kevin Downswell performance, representing a double portion of God's blessing.

The Search Continues, stretches the blessing to a new dimension. If there is ever a triple portion of blessing, this is it. In this book, Kevin goes beyond the obvious gifting of talent to sing, and the lyrics, to powerfully share the context, motivation and inspiration that attended the conception, composition and production of some memorable songs in his repertoire. I deliberately avoid the use of the word album, which is so much like what entertainers do out of purely commercial interest.

In Kevin's own words: "The Search Continues, really is about mankind seeking and pursuing God who rewards those who find him with the gift of himself". It is a love story, Kevin says, for God is also seeking us out. The use of the continuous tense suggests that this is a story that transcends this life and reaches into eternity. Each song title is like a sign-post on a journey; taking the traveler into an ever deepening, widening, expanding, yet closer relationship with the Almighty:

You make me stronger

That's enough

Calling me

If it's not you, then Lord it's nothing

Chosen

Forgiven

My closest friend

God is moving

More (says the Lord)

You are Lord

If it had not been (cover version)

When I remember

Already done

Situations

When we worship

The book is not autobiographical, for as Kevin himself says, "I don't need to go into the details of stuff that I have been through". This leaves the traveler free to seek and hopefully find a unique interpretation within the context of his or her own life experiences. It's not about Kevin Downswell, it's about God.

Sometimes poetic in its rhythmic use of language; at times dramatic as if being rendered before an audience; in part prosaic as if telling a story in everyday language; Kevin's writing style, like his music, does not limit him to a single genre. The effect is an engaging essay that seeks to both inform and persuade.

Through the lyrics of his songs, some of which have literally gone viral, Kevin Downswell artfully gives expression to his desire to come into the presence of God; just to look upon His face. The decision to use an additional medium to convey his message, via the written word, will leave an immense impact on his world-wide audience. If you are a seeker, like Kevin, you will find fuel for the journey in the pages of this useful, necessary and, in time, universal book.

Enjoy and be blessed by the ride.

Dr. Henley W. Morgan
Chairman and Overseer, Praise City Transformation Centre
Founder and Chairman Emeritus, Agency for Inner-city Renewal (AIR)
Co-founder, Institute for Social Entrepreneurship and Equity (I-SEE)
Honourary Consul General, Republic of Bottswana

Preface

Where this book began and the original motive behind its creation has evolved into a completely different body of work in the end. When I launched my second studio project (sophomore album) entitled "The Search Continues", my plan was to do a five-page booklet at the album launch to highlight where and how most of the songs had originated. I have always wanted to write books, but to be honest, I was my greatest roadblock. Every time I intended to start the process, I would convince myself that I wasn't ready. So clearly God knows how to bypass "us" to accomplish what He pleases, and eventually transform us from the inside out as we submit to Him.

While I was constructing this body of work, I still had the small booklet in mind, but then the date passed to release it, but I never stopped writing. It has metamorphosed into what you now have in your hand. The purpose behind it has also significantly expanded with time.

One of the main influences behind this book is you; yes, the one reading it right now. Oftentimes I would encounter people who, full of excitement about my songs, would ask how I wrote a particular song and where I was when I penned it. Over and over people would approach me no matter where I traveled. I observed the depth of how these songs have affected their lives and became more and more convinced that they deserved to know at least a little about the background of some of these songs. I felt as though those I had the privilege of meeting were a representation of the many others I have never encountered who wanted to know more. I also use this opportunity to expand on the scriptural background of each song and how it relates to our day-to-day lives.

While I was writing this book, my life was also changing. I was delving into an area of reaching people I thought I wasn't ready for. But God knew all along that He was orchestrating everything, and I tell you, there's no better place to be than where God wants us to be.

I normally try to be very disciplined and persistent at what I do, so when I was made privy into what God was really doing, I became excited that he wanted to accomplish something like this on a larger scale. I was no longer hesitant or doubtful of my readiness, because if God was taking the lead, He knew exactly what He was doing. This literally compelled me to keep writing. I would spend sleepless nights to ensure that I got it done and read books constantly to not just enhance my vocabulary, but to also increase my knowledge about God, the God of this book. The Bible however, has always been my main source. I would live in it day and night, meditating on its meanings and applications.

May you all come to realize that our issues and apparent limitations are only a distraction from the real thing—things used by God so we could find Him. May your search and journey to find the real you, in Him, never end until you get to the place where when you look at yourself, you only see Him. Until, then, **The Search Continues.**

YOU MAKE ME STRONGER

1.

You're my creator, Lord You know my times
Seasons of breakthrough, my seasons of trials
So I will seek you, and You I will find
You're my strong tower, in You I will hide

> *Chorus:*
> *You make me stronger*
> *Oh oh oh, oh oh oh*
> *You make me stronger, oh oh oh, oh oh oh (Repeat)*

2.

I lift my spirit; Lord I take Your hand
You've fixed my focus, now I know who I am
I used to run from battles, but You've made me strong
God strong and mighty, I AM That I AM

> *Chorus (in Spanish)*
> *"Usted me hace más fuerte"*
> *Oh oh oh, oh oh oh (Repeat)*
> *Spain (Europe), Central America (Costa Rica, Honduras, El Salvador) South America (Puerto Rico, Colombia, Bolivia, Venezuela)*

> *Chorus (in English)*
> *You make me stronger*
> *Oh oh oh, oh oh oh*
> *You make me stronger, oh oh oh, oh oh oh (Repeat)*

> *Chorus (in Swahili)*
> *Yesu Hufanya Mimi nguvu (Swahili)*
> *Oh oh oh, oh oh oh*
> *Eastern and Western Africa —Uganda, Somalia, Mozambique, Malawi, Rwanda, Burundi, Zambia, etc...*

> *Chorus (in English)*
> *You make me stronger*
> *Oh oh oh, oh oh oh*
> *You make me stronger, oh oh oh, oh oh oh (Repeat)*

CHAPTER 1

You Make Me Stronger

The Story Behind the Song

I have witnessed the world-wide response to the song, "You Make Me Stronger" and I must say, I'm lost for words and it moves me to prayer:

I pray for the thousands who have been blessed and have used this song as a tool to drive them forward and to strengthen their faith, the Lord bless you.

I pray the fire in your life and in your heart will never die as you see God's will be done on earth.

I pray the purpose of God in your hearts will be fulfilled and drawn out by people of understanding and Godly wisdom (Proverbs 20:5).

I pray for those who are going through the "rain", that you will know it will make you stronger, even if you can't see how.

I pray that you will see the omnipotent power of God in your life and that you will allow Him to qualify you for what He has already set before you. Oh that we may know Him in the fellowship of His suffering, and the power of His resurrection (Philippians 3:10).

There is a saying that God doesn't normally call the qualified, but qualifies the called. We have to know that He went ahead of us to secure the future we get so anxious about sometimes, and then He stepped back to now lead us into it. He alone knows the path we should take to tap into our greatest victories and breakthroughs.

So be still and know, He will make you stronger.

Proverbs 3 verses 5 and 6 states, "Trust in the Lord with all thy heart; and lean not unto thine own understanding. In all thy ways acknowledge him, and he shall direct thy paths." Proverbs 19 verse 21 also states, "Many are the plans in a person's heart, but it is the Lord's purpose that prevails."

I actually wrote this song originally on another beat/rhythm, a much slower one too, but when the time came to revisit it, I just could not find the recording of the beat, neither could I remember it. So, right there and then, the Lord dropped into my spirit the beat He originally intended and the rest is His-story.

I wanted to ensure that people of other languages could enjoy and identify with this song, and if I could have put all the various languages in this world into it, I would. I've received messages from around the world from people who testify that the Lord has used this song to touch their lives. From Venezuela to France, from the U.S to Australia, people all over are being impacted, all for the glory of God. Who knows, there might even be a remix with French, Hebrew and other languages quite soon. Let's see what the future holds.

You Make me Stronger. Yes, God makes us stronger.

Philippians 3 verse 13 says, "I can do all things through Christ who strengthens me".

Psalms 41 verse 11 states, "by this I know that you favor me, because my enemy does not triumph over me. Psalms 18:32-34 (same as 2 Samuels 22:33-35) says "It is God that girds me with strength, and makes my way perfect. He makes my feet like hinds' feet, and sets me upon my high places. He teaches my hands to make war, so that a bow of bronze is bent by my arms."

You Make me Stronger is a song of victory and pure glorious joy. It makes you just want to dance in the midst of your pain and turmoil, because we are reminded that all these things are working together for our good. God makes us stronger, not just for yesterday, or for today, but also for the future. He supplies something rare but so potent, that seems to pull us through the roughest and toughest of life situations.

I have been through many challenges and I'm sure you have too. Circumstances that could have destroyed me, and to tell you the truth, I am still clueless of how God brought me through. My heart overflows with praise to God whenever I think of all He has done. Someone once told me that "Conquerors" are those who fight for themselves, but those who are "more than conquerors" sit still and watch God fight for them. Well, that has proven itself true in my life over and over again.

It's quite reassuring to know that someone who is bigger, wiser, and knows all things is in control of even the weirdest things we encounter each day. It brings tremendous peace when we know our Father can never fail. He is not just in the driver's seat, but He cares more about our well-being even more than we do.

I usually tell young people that God cares more about who we become at the end of a process than the actual reward we receive. Allow God the freedom and the liberty He seeks to take us where He will. We will not regret it. We must allow Him to shape us into the image He has in mind. I personally could have been a very bitter man, but God has been with me, and He has never left. He walks with us through the toughest of times, and like a coach, teaches us how to endure hardness as a good soldier.

I don't need to go into the details about situations that I have been through because I want to emphasise the "keeping power" of Jesus Christ. Whenever soldiers are being trained for battle, inasmuch as the process to qualify is quite rigid, this process isn't normally done on a real battle ground, so there's some kind of safety involved. But when a follower of Jesus Christ is being prepared, he is placed in a real battle, to face real enemies. As tough as this may sound, both situations are different, for we have someone who fights for us. But we have to walk in obedience to His every command. As we obey God's word, we find ourselves changing; becoming all God intended us for and to be. Maybe you and I can share that feeling of thankfulness and appreciation when we see ourselves changing. We are not saved by good works, but we are saved in Christ Jesus to do good works, His work.

Christ makes me stronger, and one day without Him is a day I would never want to see. He takes me over the most insurmountable barriers, and I don't know how He does it, but He does, and that's why I love Him. I'm passionate about Him, for I have come to know Him in so many ways. "If I never had a problem, I wouldn't know he could solve them." (*Through it All lyrics* by Andraé Crouch). It is these experiences that cause us to love Him, and to never let Him go. It cements our faith, and causes us to appreciate His way of doing things. I know He watches you, I know He watches me, "for He has given His angels charge over us to keep us in all our ways" (Psalms 91:11).

He makes me stronger, better and more than a conqueror, and I will sanctify His name wherever I go. I will forever love and praise the Lord for He is good, and His grace and mercy endures forever.

(ABOVE) Kevin Downswell, in Minnesota, after delivering a powerful m inistry to the students.

(OPPOSITE) One of Downswell's signature acts is to have everyone join hands and lift them as a sign of unity and togetherness. God makes us all stronger, no matter what race, colour or background.

THAT'S ENOUGH

1.

There always somebody talking about me
But really I don't mind
They try to stop and block my progress
Most of the time
The mean things they say
Don't make me feel bad
Cause I can't miss a friend
That I never had
I got Jesus, I got Jesus
And that's enough Oh Lord, That's enough.

2.

There's been so many times
That I didn't have a dime
I tell nobody but my Lord
He heard my plea and came to see about me
He's my all and all
When they push me down, Jesus picks me up
Sticks by me when the going get tough
Take care of my enemies when they start to get rough
That's enough Oh Lord, That's enough.

> Chorus
> He saved me—that's enough; He raised me—that's enough
> He brought me—that's enough; He taught me—that's enough
> He's my shepherd He's my guide I can feel him walking by my side
> He saved me—That's enough; Keep me—That's enough
> Feed me—That's enough

3.

Prodigal Son's verse
Jesus a mi Dadda (father)
Know mi before mi madda (mother)
Never leave me, nor forsake me

Never tell me Him can't badda (bother)
With me in every weather
A Him alone me Redda (prefer)
Want get high up in him presence even if me need a ledda (ladder)
God a me break through, Him a me way maker
Set me free, Him a di chain breaker
From nutten, to the stage, to the News paper
Rescue we, now we a world changer
God a boss from earth, to the heaven to the cross
Fi di sins of di world, Jesus pay di cost
Him a di light of di world when yuh lost
That's more than enough.

    Chorus
    He saved me—that's enough; He raised me—that's enough
    He brought me—that's enough; He taught me—that's enough
    He's my shepherd, He's my guide, I can feel him walking, by my side
    He saved me—That's enough; Keep me—That's enough
    Feed me—That's enough; When I'm hungry—That's enough
    I've got Jesus, I've got Jesus; That's enough Oh Lord, That's enough.

Bridge/Vamp
He's my heart regulator, great Emancipator, Jesus is
When you refuse me, scorn me; Turn your back on me,
He's my all in all
When they push me down, Jesus picks me up
He sticks by me when the going get tough
Takes care of my enemies when they start to get rough
That's enough, Oh Lord and that's enough.

    Chorus (Repeat 3-times)
    He saved me—That's enough; Keep me—That's enough
    Feed me—That's enough; When I'm hungry—That's enough
    I've got Jesus, I've got Jesus
    That's enough Oh Lord, That's enough

CHAPTER 2

That's Enough

The Story Behind the Song

I have always wanted to do this song, but as usual, it's not me to just get up and do something spontaneous, I have to know it is what God wants me to do. In June of 2010 therefore, I felt the Lord leading me to return to do this song.

You see, when I think about it, I was not at the right place to deliver this song. So though I had the desire, it wasn't God's time. I hope that says something to someone who has been anxious to do certain things for God. You see my friend, not every good idea is a "God" Idea.

The minute I knew that God showed me the open door, I ran forward. I approached Haldane "Danny" Brownie, and for those who know this man, will concur that he is a genius. He took the song from an idea to what it is today.

I collaborated with one of Jamaica's most gifted gospel artiste, Calvin Whilby (Prodigal Son), who did a marvelous job. Collaborations are supposed to be the merging of two or more strong points. One person might be weak in one area, but that might be the other's strength, so in the end, the product should be exceptional, especially when God is in it. This is exactly what happened.

Now, something interesting happened when the song was completed.

After picking up the finished product from Brownie, and I was on my way from his studio, I turned on my car radio and a program was on talking about Mephibosheth from the Bible. Read 2 Samuel 4:4; 2 Samuel 9; 2 Samuel 19:24-30 and 2 Samuel 21:1-7. Jonathan (Saul's son) had a son named Mephibosheth, who was crippled as a child. He was five years old when the report came from Jezreel that Saul and Jonathan (Mephibosheth's father) had been killed in battle. When the child's nurse heard the news, she picked him up and fled. But as she hurried away, she dropped him, and he became crippled.

A long time passed and David wanted to show kindness to anyone of Saul's descendants who was still alive. This happened to be Mephibosheth, who by now must have felt forgotten and forlorn, and who interestingly lived in a place called Lo-debar (meaning "no pasture" or "barren"). In brief, Mephibosheth who seemed to have been forgotten, was promoted and given all the land that belonged to his grandfather Saul and ate at the King's table.

Let me stop here to say, God has not forgotten you. It might have been a long, long time that you have been trodding on "Waiting Avenue", but the God that I know never forgets. Psalms 56 verse 8 states, "Record my misery; list my tears on your scroll—are they not in your record?" it goes on to say, "by this I know that God is for me".

I did not get the chance to listen to the entire programme, but all I remember are the two words "sought" and "brought". You see, the Lord used that programme to really bring home this song to me. Like Mephibosheth, we were in a terrible state—I was in a terrible state. And some terrible things happened to us. Some of us got written off by people. For some of us, the very people we were counting on in the first place to have our backs, let us down.

David said in Psalms 55 verses 12-14, "If an enemy were insulting me I could endure it; if a foe were rising against me, I could hide. But it is you, a man like myself, my companion, my close friend, with whom I once enjoyed sweet fellowship at the house of God, as we walked about among the worshipers." But God in all His mercy sought after us. He combed through all the mess and dirt. You see, we can never be too messed up that God can't find us and take the mess and make us His message to the rest of the world. Satan comes to steal and to wreck us, but not God. His plan is to restore and bring us into what was originally ours and to cause us to eat from His table.

Like Mephibosheth who was lame in both feet, I was helpless. I could not do much all by myself, BUT GOD.... The very land God restored to Mephibosheth, David had to fight for it, but not Mephibosheth, It was his. Jesus is everything and more. We don't need to struggle against flesh and blood.

We shall recover all, and like Israel and Canaan, even if someone currently occupies something God promised you, When God is ready, you shall have it.

Be still and know that He is God.

As Mephibosheth was humble before the king, let's remember that it is He who brought us out, and blessed us and not ourselves.

This song *That's Enough* is my testimony and your testimony of God's unfailing love and goodness.

Young people are naturally drawn to the presence of God. Here Downswell is delivering "That's Enough" before hundreds of young people.

Kevin Downswell's impact spans generations. Seen here with an elderly woman dancing on stage to "That's Enough", during ministry in May Pen, Clarendon, Jamaica.

Prodigal Son (RIGHT), who collaborated with Downswell on "That's Enough", stands with him as both are being ministered to.

CALLING ME *(Featuring Papa Son)*

Chorus
Calling me to a higher place; Calling me to a higher level
I wanna go to a higher place, I wanna go to a higher level

1.
Keeping my eyes fixed on the prize; I will not be denied
Devil trying to push me to the left and the right; But I will not even blink one eye
Focus I am gonna get there; Until me Jesus Christ become the perfect pair,
Two becoming one; Lord I lift my hands I surrender all

2.
A Him set me straight when mi poor and naked
Fill me with love when mi wicked and wretched
Forgive me of my sins and brush off and call me blessed
Enlarge my territories like mi friend weh name Jabez
With mi hands stretched forth, and my face hit the floor
Then You start talk to me, about the blessing of the poor
A You have the remedy the cure
Take me to the secret place Jesus You a di door
Move every chain and every shackle
A You fight mi battle; please take me to Your tabernacle (God)
In the beauty of Your Holiness, when I'm here I will find rest

Bridge
I'm coming up—inna mi prayer and mi devotion
I'm coming up—3mi obedience and mi submission
I'm coming up—You no stop show mi favor
I'm coming up—tell mi seh mi haffi love mi neighbor
I'm coming up—When mi gone pan mi knees mi God
I'm coming up—My Lord a beg You please my God
I'm coming up—I will never stop serve You
I'm coming up—You love me when I don't deserve You

Repeat Chorus

CHAPTER 3

Calling Me
The Story Behind the Song

I've always possessed a high level of respect for gospel artiste, Tyrone Thompson (Papa Son, formerly Papa San). His impact worldwide through the calling of God on his life is tremendous. His experience goes deep and whenever we dialogue, I take every opportunity to learn from the wisdom that pours from him.

When I wrote this song, *Calling Me,* I knew, without a doubt, that he was the one to collaborate with. Let me also add that my manager, Wendell Lawrence, produced this track, a job well done. When he introduced me to it, the words came without effort. At the time of writing this song, my heart was focused on us as a church and on how ready we are to being God's perfect bride.

God is a God of seasons and like the four seasons we have each year, summer, autumn, winter, spring, they all change. So in our Christian walk with God, we must be aware that at some point, we are going to be required to "grow up". No human being who started life as a child, stays as a child for the rest of their earthly life. So we must expect the beckoning call to transition from one level to another in God as well.

But what are we really expected to grow in? The first thing that comes to most of our minds is that we all need to either pray longer; spend more time in worship and studying the Bible or go to church more often. But I believe this song is saying much more than that. For so many times we focus on the more apparent and traditional areas of Christianity, and don't realize that God might be asking us to either love the ones in our lives who we can't seem to tolerate or maybe it's to forgive and let go of someone who has hurt us in the past. Maybe it's our obedience to God's instructions. Whatever it is, God is saying something right now to someone, which carries so much weight, our entire future depends on it. Will we care to listen?

Whatever God is saying to you might be something totally the opposite He is asking of me, so it's important for each and every one of us to make every effort to hear God and respond. The quicker we respond, the quicker His purpose behind these requests are fulfilled. It's like a student, who studies for an exam. He spends time with the tutor learning and absorbing all the knowledge he needs so that when final exam comes around, he will be ready. Well, if when the test is sat, the student fails, then he can't move on from the level he is at and will not be elevated or promoted until he meets all the requirements for that promotion.

Well, so it is with God.

We study His word and spend time in His amazing presence soaking up His love, strength, wisdom and revelations. But normally when it's time for us to be promoted, He introduces a test. Now the Bible clearly states that God tempts no man nor can He be tempted, but what He does is allow it and, if we pass, we receive the reward and an automatic promotion to another level in Him. But if we fail, we will remain at that level until we really get it right.

I don't want to be stuck at any level for too long if God has been calling me higher. I want to soar, higher, and higher in Him. At the end of every test is a reward; at the end of every test is a better you too; for when we respond to God's gentle nudge to come up higher, the process to get there makes us more like Him.

The word declares in Ephesians 2:10 that "We are God's workmanship, created in Christ Jesus to do good works, which God prepared in advance for us to do" (emphasis added).

My friend, do not delay any longer. One of the greatest obstacles to progress is lack of focus. Wherever you are in your life, you know God is calling you higher, to become better, like the Nike slogan suggests, "Just do it".

Aren't you curious of what lies ahead? Will you settle for crumbs when you can have the whole thing?

Find yourself around people who starve your fleshly cravings, but challenge your Godly pursuits. You can do all things through Christ who gives you strength (Philippians 3:13). I quote that verse of Scripture because some of us have failed so many times in one area that we seem to have accepted defeat. We don't have the faith like we used to, and no longer believe God can cause us to beat this thing, succumbing to the deception that "this is who I am". Well, this is not the truth. You are what God's words say you are. If it's not in the Bible, do not accept it. Do not settle for less in this life. Get to work, and remember, it is God that does the changing in you; your part is to allow Him to do it. So many times we get worked up trying to live for God when all we have to simply do is allow God to do His work in us.

Rise like an eagle; soar with the wind of God. Lose yourself in the currents of His flow.

He calls us, not with compulsion, but through the glory of His excellent greatness. Our hearts say yes Lord, we rise up higher, we sacrifice greater, we live louder.

Parents contact Downswell telling him that their children are in love with his songs. They smile and share a laugh that they can't play any other music in the car when their children are with them.

Downswell leading persons to Christ—a central aspect of his ministry.

An aerial photo showing Downswell and his band delivering "Calling Me" at Liberation 2013.

IF IT'S NOT YOU (then Lord it's nothing)

1.

I'm searching; I won't stop till I find...You
I'm running, I won't stop till I touch...You
You're my destination, You're all I got
Nothing can deter me, I said I won't stop

> *Chorus*
> *If it's not You, then Lord it's nothing*
> *If it's not You, it's nothing at all*
> *If it's not You, then Lord it's nothing*
> *It's got to be You*

2.

Lord I love You, because You first loved me
The height, the depth, the length, the breadth of Your love, set me free
So I give You everything, no holding back
My heart is Yours Lord, cause it's all I've got

Bridge
When we seek You, we shall find You, when we have searched with all our hearts.
One day with You, is more than a thousand elsewhere,
Lord we draw near.

CHAPTER 4

If it's not You

The Story Behind the Song

So many individuals have approached me and have asked me where was I when I penned this song, as they expressed how celestial the words are. It is such a blessing when a song which was originally the expression of your heart to God can become cherished and loved by so many other people. The song reached those who were trying to formulate the words of how to just let God know how they love Him, but this song couldn't say it any better. This is truly humbling, and we give thanks to the King of kings.

Well, I was on tour in Canada in the summer of 2011, and things were not really going my way. I was getting anxious and worried that I wouldn't fulfill all my intentions for which I had set out to accomplish. But then I had a couple of days to rest, and that's when God spoke. He simply asked me to come away with Him, a request to which I quickly complied.

I had access to an old broken Yamaha keyboard which I used to practice my piano lessons, and I was in worship, just pouring out my heart to God, tears running down, I was totally broken...and there in that moment, God spoke. He said gently, "Kevin, sing to me...." He went on to reassure me that He knew how I felt but all He would like to hear is what my heart is saying. So, in the midst of me feeling disappointment based on how things were going, in the midst of my "Lo-debar" experience, the words of this song flowed from my heart.

It was a bold declaration that nothing really mattered but Him. I wasn't throwing my hands up in defeat, it was me throwing my hands up in complete surrender to the One who controlled the battle and ultimately the outcome of the wars we wage daily. It was an all or nothing stance, and I knew He felt it, I knew it, cause right there and then, His presence filled my space so much that I froze, unable to play another key or utter another word. Only tears of worship, and so it all changed after this, where my heart was re-positioned in a place of true order. I didn't doubt Him anymore; I pressed forward confidently knowing He was with me and that He was in charge.

You see, this song encompasses so many areas in life. It is an enactment of Psalms 42:1, and is an active pursuit for the One whom we know we can't live without. These days, men have decided they don't need God, because they think they have all they need, but only he who is thirsty will go get water, only He who is hungry will go seek for food. If we don't have a passion, we won't seek.

It's a bold declaration that every decision, every contract signed, every deal accepted or rejected, if God is not in it, the answer is no. It's boldly taking a stand in these compromising days, to not accept anything that does not have the signature of Christ on it.

It's also a love song, "one day with You is more than a thousand elsewhere, Lord we draw near."

"As the deer pants for the water brook, so my soul pants for You oh God. My soul thirsts for You oh God, When can I come and meet with God"(Psalms 42:1,2).

The interesting thing in seeking God is that even though we seek—it's God's initiative to respond. Like David, our insatiable passion for God should not allow us to stop until we are caught by Him, until we gain the one after whom we seek. It's intentional, and most of the times not innate, for our flesh will always say we don't need to ask, or seek Him. But how could I not seek the only One who sees my future in moving ahead? How could I not seek the Omniscient God who knows my end from the beginning?

Sometimes we are much too comfortable to expend the effort such a passion requires. The reason people don't seek Him with such passion could be that we have not experienced the beauty and awesomeness of God's manifested presence, Hence, we don't understand that the reward for seeking is worth every bit of our effort and sacrifice.

I don't know if you have ever been at a place where it was God's input that made all the difference. And if He did not speak, or manifest, our lives would not have been where it is right now. If He didn't lead you to make the right decision in that area, making the wrong move would have been devastating. His grace is sufficient to keep us. David comes to mind, when he was about to fight the Philistines. He asked God if he should go up against them.

It's realizing that I cannot do without Him. Firstly, God's presence is everything and when His presence is revealed, He releases: (i) His wisdom. I'm not wise enough to make any decision without Him. (ii) His love and peace—I'm not able to stay calm enough when stuff goes wrong. My world is always changing, but because He is and always is firm and unmovable; with Him, I am stabilized. As a result, I am constantly seeking Him, for He is all I'll ever need.

If it's not God, who is my healer, my companion and the centre of my life, then nothing else will do. My heart, the seat of all my emotions, affections, desires, passion, love and all other feelings cannot survive without Him. You see, that's where all my ideas and thoughts come from. My heart dictates my behavior, my conduct and my attitude. I seek and serve God with all my heart so that He has complete control over my emotions, decisions, and thoughts in my life. We all know the enemy never ceases from trying to corrupt what God created for His glory.

It's in Him we find strength; it's in Him we overcome.

In my closing, I tell people all the time that seeking God is not about stuff, but all about Him. When we make it about material things, we lose the things we ask for because we fail to gain the presence of the One who holds them in His hands. Lord I'm building a house for You with my praise, but it's empty if You don't move in.

Praise is us building a house for God, worship is God moving in.

We may seek God through praise, but it is up to God whether He will respond to our initiative. Moses cried in Exodus 33:15, "Lord if Your presence doesn't go with us, don't let us go up from here. It was David who also said, "You have made known to me the path of Life…In your presence there is fullness of Joy, at your right hand pleasures for evermore."

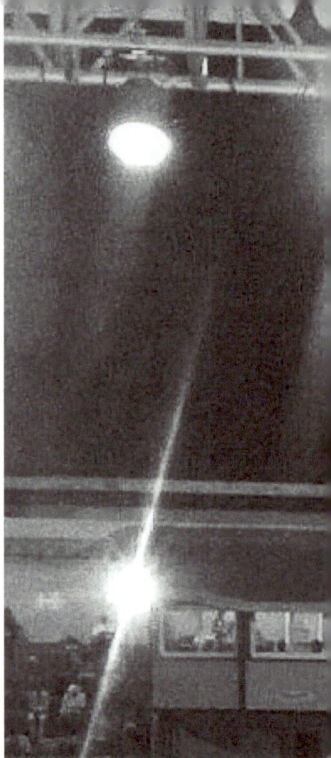

(OPPOSITE) Kevin Downswell delivering a life changing song "If It's Not You", with a powerful message in St. Vincent and the Grenadines. This song is an anthem to many across the world.

(BELOW) The students of Manchester High School with their hands outstretched to God as Minister Downswell delivers "If it's Not You".

CHOSEN

Chorus
I'm chosen, by You
I'm chosen, by You
I'm chosen by You, who make all the things new
I'm chosen, chosen, chosen by You
(Chosen by You, chosen by You)

1.

My heart door is open
Lion of Judah hosanna, hosanna,
You gave me new song,
You've made me Your dwelling place
I'm not worthy, but I humbly accept,
I'm not worthy, still You choose to bless

Chorus
I'm chosen, by You
I'm chosen, by You
I'm chosen by You, who make all the things new
I'm chosen, chosen, chosen by You
(Chosen by You, chosen by You)

2.

When I think of all I've done,
How could I be Your chosen one?
When I think of all the mess I've made in my life
It's hard to believe I'm still Your choice
It blows my mind; I'm Yours You are mine
I give You glory, All the glory...

Bridge
You've changed my destiny
I 'm chosen to bring You glory
While I was just a servant You called me a king
I was an outcast, but You called me friend

CHAPTER 5

Chosen

The Story Behind the Song

I remember the special day this song "dropped" on me. I was driving from one appointment to the other. I was on my way to record a particular song, and right there on Winchester Avenue, near Half Way Tree, in Kingston, Jamaica, I was compelled to pull over on the soft shoulder. I just could not go any further, as the words, the tune; I mean everything was being deposited in my system all at once.

I began to write, and completely forgot that I was perched on the soft shoulder of the road. Suddenly I looked up and saw a few pedestrians trying to squeeze past the vehicle to continue on to their destination. I was obviously blocking them, and some were not happy at all. So with an anxious grin on my face, I beckoned to them my apologies and quickly went back to complete the song. This was truly a joyous moment, as I had already felt the virtue of this song and knew it would be a blessing to many.

The message: *We are chosen by God.*

This revelation is priceless, and it shatters every lie and cunning deception of the enemy, lifting us to a place of prominence even if subsequent to knowing this, we find ourselves still living in a shack. Once we truly discover that we are chosen by God, we'll instantaneously begin to pursue Him so as to know why He chose us. We'll be infused with such passion and drive to excel and never dwell in passivity any longer.

It will cause the one who should have been immersed in utter sadness based on their circumstances, to be able to crack a smile, knowing that God chose them. It will bring confidence and identity to the one who has been ostracized and rejected by society, because of some physical disability or educational disadvantage.

We are not talking about being chosen by the prime minster or the president of a particular country, we are talking about the One who placed them in power. The

King of Kings, the Lord of Lords. The president extraordinaire and His name is Jesus Christ. Truth of this caliber can quicken the dead, bringing them to life. So many people were on the path to excellence and success, but messed up along the way, but this song reminds us that with God, it's never too late.

"While I was just a servant, he called me a king", Wow! To the Chinese, the Asian, the African, the Caucasian, the Indian, the Jamaican, the Puerto Rican and the likes, yes, He searched high and low, just to get to you.

And the thing is, most of us had no idea that Someone thought of us with such intent and focus, and believed in us. I am quite guilty, for sometimes I consider myself detached and undeserving of God's goodness, Yet, He relentlessly presses in, declaring that I'm the one He chooses. It makes you wonder what we did to sanction such favor. Well.... Nothing. For the word declares we could do nothing to earn God's love. It's not of works that any should boast (Ephesians 2:9), He loves me unconditionally. This eliminates doubts and fears. It makes you want to hold your head high. For to be chosen by God is the highest call anyone could ever receive, the most prestigious award.

If He chose me, therefore, it only means that I am chosen for something, since God does nothing without a reason. He does nothing without having prefigured in His mind what it is and what He intended it to be. So when things seem to not be going your way, let us be at peace, for God's power is unmatched.

Like David, even if you do not look the part, you're the one. You might have been born in a family that has an unfortunate history or circumstances, well God might have chosen you to rewrite all that, and set a new precedence for the next generation through you.

Whether you are in a wheel chair or use prosthetics to move around, you are chosen by God. And I think it's time for us to seek Him with the same passion with which He sought after us. All things were made by Him for Him, so don't get lost in this big world wondering what's the big idea. Wherever He is, that's the direction you should head into.

Why you?

Well, God has a reputation of using the unassuming to humble the great, the foolish things to confound the wise, the underdogs to rise up as victors. Have you even been underestimated? Have you ever been considered unworthy to partake in something you knew you should have been a part of but kept out by man's unwillingness to see the difference in you?

Grace, the grace of God, is what this song is about. "While we were yet sinners, Christ died for us" (Romans 5:1-10). While we were not thinking about Him, He could not take His mind off us. Oh what love, I just cannot comprehend it. I will be ever grateful, for God loved me even when He knew how sinful and wayward I was. We praise You Father, thank You for choosing us.

When someone is chosen by God, we must understand that the purpose existed before the act of choosing. Which means God chose us for a particular purpose. He called us to a particular mandate. So I pray for every woman, every man, who has been lied to and deceived by Satan, that the eyes of your understanding will be enlightened that you will discover the depth of God's love and the purpose of your choosing, and how to please the One who called you by name.

God cannot make mistakes; you were separated by Him, to do what no one else can; to fit that space of the puzzle no one else has the ability to occupy. When you were born and cried your first cry, heaven knew your sound. Satan goes after the gifted because he knows if you discover who you are in God, he will be powerless against you. You are chosen by God. If God approves of you, no man can disqualify you. Whether you have the education or not, the experience or not, if God says it, that settles it.

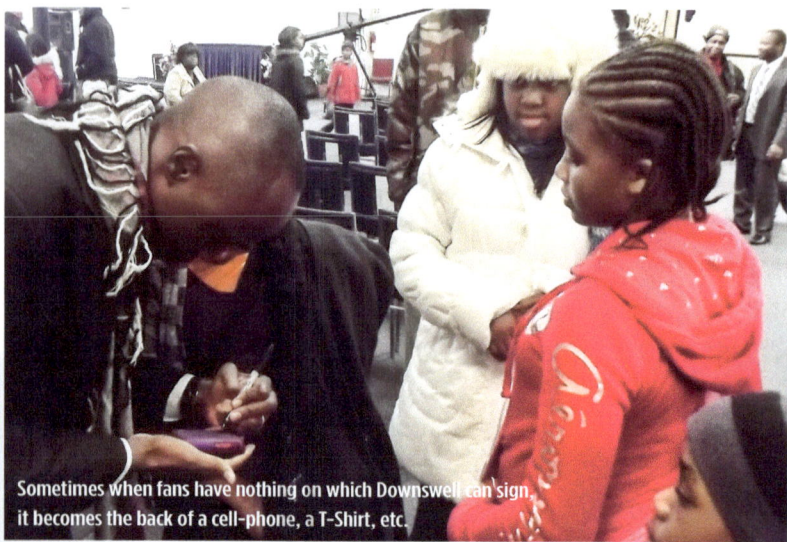

Sometimes when fans have nothing on which Downswell can sign, it becomes the back of a cell-phone, a T-Shirt, etc.

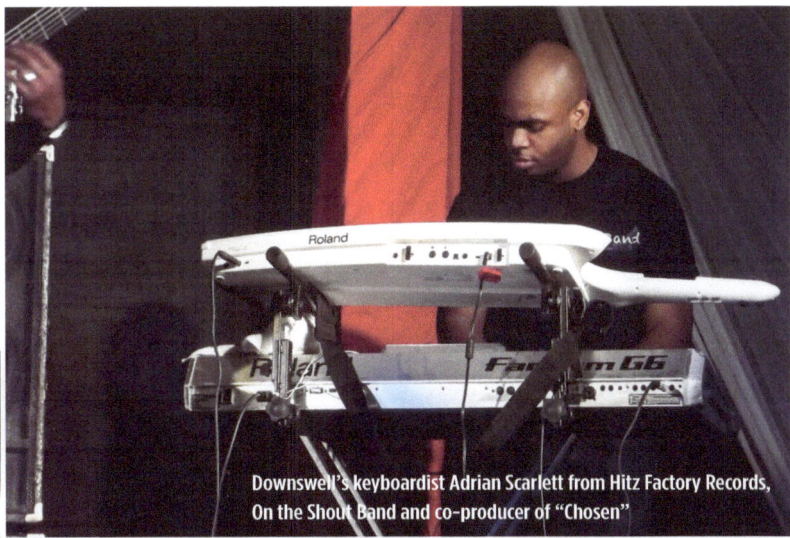

Downswell's keyboardist Adrian Scarlett from Hitz Factory Records, On the Shout Band and co-producer of "Chosen"

Downswell with hands lifted delivering "Chosen".

FORGIVEN

Chorus
I never knew, that being forgiven would be so right
I never knew, that Your love would change my life
I am a new creature; old things are past away,
Past away, gone away, now my soul will bless Your name

1.
Can I tell you about the One who saved my soul?
I can't keep still my brother I'm finally on the right road
My mother used to say He would walk with me,
But right now, He even talks with me
I have a testimony how He rescued me, I wanna tell you, can I tell you?

2.
God of Abraham, God of Isaac, God of Jacob
There's no coincidence why I'm here,
I'm reminding you that He cares
He's been with me through my darkest hour
When my enemies came against me to devour
But I'm still here; He kept me from their snares

Bridge
I'm free, Free like a bird in the sky
I'm free, Spread my wings and fly
I'll sour, like an eagle, higher,
Lord it's because of you
Without you what would I do?

Vamp
Somebody knows what I'm talking about
My past is gone away, Jesus is here to stay
When I have no words to say, this is all I've got to say
Oh oh, oh oh oh(repeat)
Oooh, oooh , oooh oooh oooh (repeat)

CHAPTER 6

Forgiven
The Story Behind the Song

Something quite miraculous took place from the very inception of this song.

It was the first song I released as a single to commence activities surrounding my sophomore album. It came at the time when I felt God had lifted me to a new spiritual position. So my eyes were opened to new things, fresh approaches and endless possibilities. I began to receive unusual revelations of the word forgiveness, the privilege that we have as mankind to be redeemed by the shed blood of Jesus Christ. My eyes were being opened to a deeper understanding of God's love. So I decided to pen my experience.

Tears flowed from my eyes every time I entered His presence as I reminisced of God's grace and mercy. Romans 5:9-11 states "Since we have now been justified by his blood, how much more shall we be saved from God's wrath through him. For if, while we were God's enemies, we were reconciled to Him through the death of His Son, how much more, having been reconciled, shall we be saved through His life! Not only is this so, but we also boast in God through our Lord Jesus Christ, through whom we have now received reconciliation."

"I never knew that being forgiven would be so right." That's the first line in the chorus. It sounds like a strange way of putting it, but no matter how I tried to phrase it differently, nothing else would fit. I knew this was the Lord trying to let me know that it was perfect as it is.

After writing this song, and getting ready to find musicians to assemble the track, I eventually found myself one day, sitting with Wendell Lawrence, my manager. I took the paper out, and began to sing the tune to him. I was only a few lines into the verse when my manager jumped up and said, "but hold on, that tune sounds exactly like a track I've been working on". Well, so said so done. I wrote the words and configured the tune in my own private time, and he constructed the musical track in his private time. We had no dialogue, or any prior communication, but we found ourselves in complete awe of God's awesomeness, as it all came together. We lifted our hands in praise to the All-knowing God, for He was the one behind all this.

"Forgiven" is a powerful song, and it was the first track to be released for my second album, which was to be named "The Search Continues".

Let me try to put this song in the context in regards to how I think we are to love God, and how we are to approach Him.

The word declares that—"There is no fear in love, but perfect love casts out fear. For fear has to do with punishment, and he who fears is not perfected in love" (1 John 4:18). Where there is fear, unholy fear, true love cannot exist.

If there is any presence of fear in the heart, love cannot be openly displayed. The fear of punishment will automatically disqualify the one who has it from genuinely loving the one he fears. All his service towards that person will be done with the purpose of alleviating the wrath of that person towards him. Such service, therefore, springs not from love but from self-motivation. The man who serves God because he has no assurance of forgiveness from God, and seeks by this service to obtain that forgiveness, has his own welfare at heart. He most certainly does not truly love God, for love is selfless.

Love, as a motivation of the heart, knows no partners. For love to be genuine there cannot be any other factor affecting the service of the one who seeks to express that love.

Accordingly, if a man would serve God and keep his commandments through genuine love, there may not be any fear of God's wrath in his heart. This makes it essential, from the outset, for there to be complete knowledge of forgiveness in the heart of the man who would to serve God out of love. That forgiveness must be experienced now, and may not be an uncertain prospect at a time to come in the future.

If a man is unsure of God's complete remission of his sins and if he does not enjoy a state of permanent forgiveness for all that he may think or does, he cannot possibly serve God out of genuine love. Though he professes love towards God, he must really serve him with the primary objective of obtaining his forgiveness and alleviating his wrath. Such service, as we have seen, is principally self-motivated as it seeks approval for itself rather than the glory of God. Therefore, if we are to truly love God, we must first experience the perfect knowledge of His forgiveness in our hearts. For our love to be genuine, a condition of complete peace with God must reign within us.

In serving Christ, the One, true living God, once He has forgiven us we can boldly enter into the Holiest by the blood of the Lamb.

We can come with joy, knowing we are free, knowing we are forgiven, and knowing that He is not listening out for the slightest flaw or mistake so He can judge us or condemn us. "There is now no condemnation to them that are in Christ who walk not after the flesh but after the Spirit" (Romans 8:1).

So let us rejoice and be glad. Let the redeemed of the Lord say so, who God has redeemed from the hands of the enemy, oppression, and bondage (Psalms 107:2-Paraphrased).

I'm free, I'm forgiven. Free from sin, and free to step into the glorious will of Yeshuah Ha' Mashiach (Hebrew for Jesus Christ).

Wendell Lawrence, Downswell's Drummer, Manager and Producer for the Track "Forgiven".

Downtown Kingston as Downswell
and his team minister on stage.

MY CLOSEST FRIEND *(Featuring Sean Lypher)*

1.

I fell on my face just the other day
If some of my so—called friends found out maybe they woulda said
"Drop him" wi no need him"
But I ran to the "Friend of all friends"
His arms were wide open
He picked me up and put me back together again.

> *Chorus*
> *He's my Closest Friend; With me to the end*
> *He's my Closest Friend; With me to the end*

2.

When you come in from work
And you feel so stressed out
And you just wanna pour it out
Call His name
When you come in from school
And you just didn't have a good day
And you have so much to say
Call Him

Vamp
If you know He's alright
If you know He's there in your midnight
If you know He's the One who'll never leave your side
If you know without Him you coulda been dead
He's the lifter of your head
He gives us courage to rise again

Sean Lypher

> *Repeat Chorus*

CHAPTER 7

My Closest Friend

The Story Behind the Song

Many of us have, in some way or another, been let down by someone who called themselves our friend. But there is One who will never fail to be faithful as a friend. Let me introduce Him to you if you don't already know Him.

His name is Jesus Christ.

He dwelt in heaven as God, King over the universe, Almighty and Omnipotent. He could have stayed there, but He saw how much you and I were in need of a Saviour. I could not have saved myself, or set myself free from what held me bound, so He came to earth, born of a virgin named Mary, just for you and me.

He lived to die for us. That was His mandate, so that we could be saved. But that was not the end of it. Because on the third day He arose, champion over the grave, and over death. "Oh death, where is your sting? Oh grave where is your victory?" (1 Corinthians 15:55).

Before He left the earth, He gave you and I the privilege to be His friend, His companion for life, so He left us His Holy Spirit, the Comforter, to lead us into all truth. The truth of who we really are in Him, that we are His, and the rights that were restored us through His coming.

Today, the things His Spirit has shown me have caused a complete change in my life. Issues like low self-esteem, oppression and bondage are no longer a part of me, for He has revealed to me just who I am. If my ancestors made a certain mistake in their lives, I don't have to repeat it, for He has taken me in, and redirected my path.

I am His friend, and He is my closest friend. There is no one else that does it quite like He does. His voice makes all the difference in my life, and I must admit that I cannot live without Him.

The Word says, "there are "friends" who destroy each other, but a real friend sticks closer than a brother" (Proverbs 18:24). And, "Never will I leave you; never will I forsake you." So we say with confidence, "The Lord is my helper, I will not be afraid. What can man do to me? (Hebrews 13:5, 6). These two Bible references help us to see that no matter what image we have of a friend, Jesus is the epitome of a true friend.

His Holy Spirit, the Comforter, never leaves us lonely. He is not just a friend; He is my closest friend, which means it's Him I go to first with my issues when I am stressed. He never condemns me, but loves me for who I am. I share with Him all of my fears and I don't just love Him, I like being with Him. He never encourages my wrong, but challenges me to be the best I was created to be. Faithful are His wounds (Proverbs 27:6) for I trust His correction knowing that He loves me unconditionally. I hope you discover what a perfect Friend the Holy Spirit is! What a Guide, what a Teacher, what a Friend.

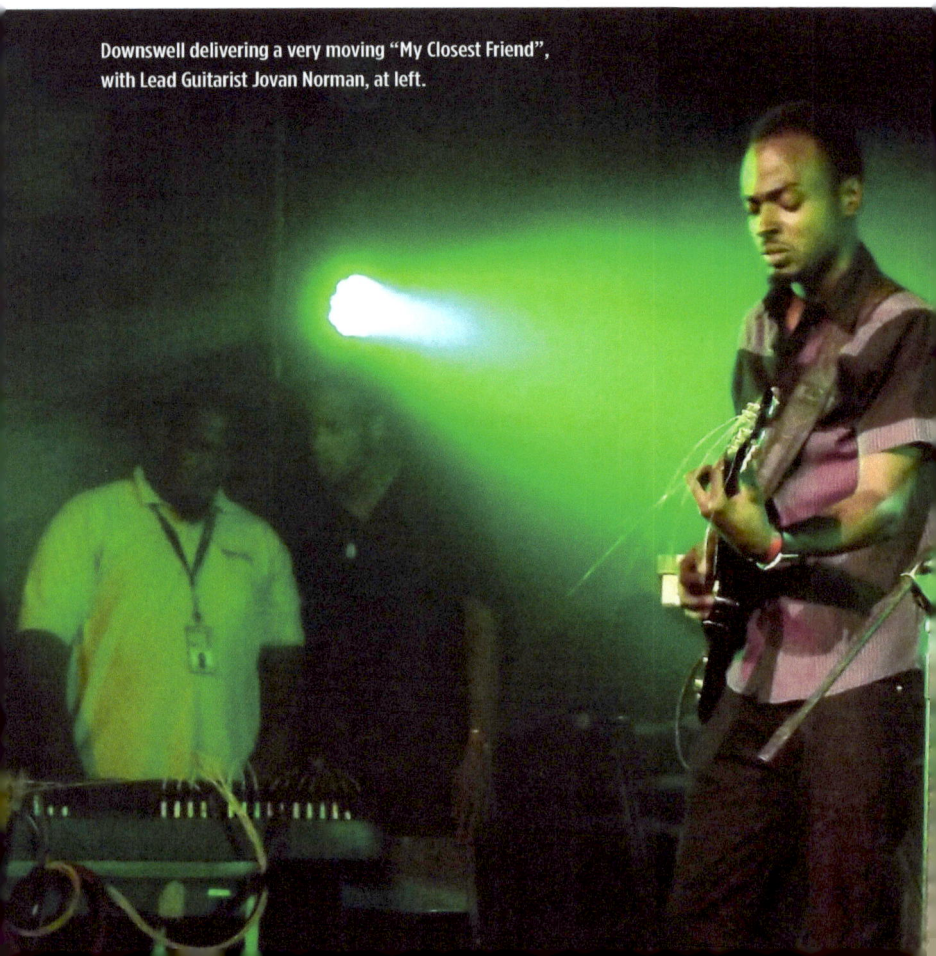

Downswell delivering a very moving "My Closest Friend", with Lead Guitarist Jovan Norman, at left.

If you have read this and felt like you want Jesus Christ to be your friend, just simply say:

> Jesus, forgive me, of all my sins. I know I am a sinner, and only You can save me. I believe that You died for me and that You were raised from the dead on the third day for me. I confess You to be my Lord and Friend as of this moment. Lord, show me how to love You, and help me to be the best friend I could ever be to You. Amen.

Welcome! You are now officially saved, now one day at a time, seek after Him. Find a good Bible-based church that will help you know more about how to draw closer to Christ. Get a Bible, for it is now your manual on how to live for Christ.

Now, you are about to see for yourself what it means to have a true friend.

Let me close by saying thanks be to God for Sean Lypher, who did this song with me, a brother with an extraordinary gift. I truly appreciate you man of God.

GOD IS MOVING

1.
There is a remnant, called by His name
Eyes have not seen, ears have not heard, the power they carry inside.
On the potter's wheel, being prepared, And though they're tested and tried,
Their victory is sure.

Vamp
All Creation waits in desperation; They know there's got to be more
While the move of God's glory is set into motion; Be ready, prepare your hearts.

Chorus
God is moving, be ready for His Glory; God is moving, be ready for His Glory,
Ready or not, no one can stop the move of God in the earth; God is moving.

2.
Satan is busy trying to steal your attention, For if you discover who you are in God,
No demon can keep you bound.
Something is happening, a mighty awakening,Let the weak say I'm strong, let the
poor say I'm rich; Order is coming to God's house.

Vamp
All Creation waits in desperation, They know there's got to be more.
While the move of God's glory is set into motion. Be ready, prepare your hearts.

Repeat Chorus

Bridge
Oh, oh, oh, oh, when the rain falls ; He who is ready, to him it will be a blessing
If the rain falls and we're not ready, We will be washed away...

Repeat Chorus

Get your house in order, for what God is doing; no man can stop it...
Lord whatever you're doing, don't do it without me,
Don't do it without Kevin.
God Is Moving

CHAPTER 8

God is Moving
The Story Behind the Song

I sat at my window one morning meditating, and the voice of the Lord instructed me to write. I immediately began not knowing where He would lead me. These are the words that came to me. At the end of writing this song, I felt an indescribable weight of the anointing on me, and I knew immediately that these words would speak life and had a very important assignment embedded within its lines. This was the third and last single released before the launch of "The Search Continues", and I've come to humbly realize that every time and everywhere I've sung it, the glory of God manifests.

It is very important for us to know and remember that God is Moving on the earth today, in our personal lives and on the global scale. Someone, somewhere at this particular moment is walking a path of testing. But it is necessary for us all to understand that God causes all things to work together for our good, to those who love Him and are called according to His purpose. Your Redeemer God says:

> Sing, barren woman, who has never had a baby. Fill the air with song, you who've never experienced childbirth! You're ending up with far more children than all those childbearing women.

> Clear lots of ground for your tents! Make your tents large. Spread out! Think big! Use plenty of rope, drive the tent pegs deep. You're going to need lots of elbow room for your growing family. You're going to take over whole nations; you're going to resettle abandoned cities.

> Don't be afraid—you're not going to be embarrassed.

> Don't hold back—you're not going to come up short. You'll forget all about the humiliations of your youth, and the indignities of being a widow will fade from memory. For your Maker is your bridegroom, his name, God-of-the-Angel-Armies! Your Redeemer is The Holy of Israel, known as God of

the whole earth. You were like an abandoned wife, devastated with grief, and God welcomed you back, like a woman married young and then left.

Your Redeemer God continues to say:

I left you, but only for a moment. Now, with enormous compassion, I'm bringing you back. In an outburst of anger I turned my back on you— but only for a moment. It's with lasting love that I'm tenderly caring for you.

This exile is just like the days of Noah for me: I promised then that the waters of Noah would never again flood the earth. I'm promising now no more anger,   no more dressing you down. For even if the mountains walk away and the hills fall to pieces, My love won't walk away from you, my covenant commitment of peace won't fall apart."   The God who has compassion on us says so.

The afflicted city, storm-battered: I'm about to rebuild you with stones of turquoise, Lay your foundations with sapphires, construct your towers with rubies, your gates with jewels, and all your walls with precious stones.

All your children will have God for their teacher—what a mentor for your children!

You'll be built solid, grounded in righteousness, far from any trouble— nothing to fear!   Far from terror—it won't even come close! If anyone attacks you, don't for a moment suppose that I sent them, and if any should attack, nothing will come of it. I create the blacksmith who fires up his forge and makes a weapon designed to kill. I also create the destroyer—but no weapon that can hurt you has ever been forged. Any accuser who takes you to court will be dismissed as a liar. This is what God's servants can expect.   I'll see to it that everything works out for the best (Isaiah 54. MSG).

This is God's message to us. He is the King of Kings, the Creator of the whole earth, who is in charge of each and everything that takes place today. Have faith in Him. We may have seen God do great and marvelous things in the past, but it's not over, for what He is planning to unfold today and tomorrow, no one has ever dreamed it. So let us be alert and make use of every time we have to be in the right place with God. Search our own hearts and see if there is any wicked thing in us.

When you feel weary and tired, find yourself back at His feet, in His presence, for He will refresh you, He will calm your fears, and redirect your steps. "The steps of a good man are ordered by the Lord" (Psalms 37:23).

I remember when God used the prophet Elijah, in 2nd Chronicles, to prophesy to Jeroboam that he would be head of ten tribes and the son of Solomon would be head over only two. Many things took place afterwards. For example, Rehoboam, the son of Solomon wanted to go up against Jeroboam to reclaim his lost ten tribes, but what the Lord had already written could not be undone, so the Lord again sent a prophet to warn Rehoboam to not go up, and thank God he did obey, for God watches over His word to perform it (Jeremiah 1:12).

Stay in God's will; take to heart His every whisper. I don't want to ever be a spectator to the move of God on the earth. God is moving. And just like Elijah, do not be confused about which move is God-initiated, for if you only stay in His will, you will make no mistake. God Is Moving, ready or not, no one can stop, the move of God in the earth, God is Moving.

Downswell's background singers from left Kerry-Ann Hinds, Sheldon Williams and Taneika Thompson.

Downswell delivering "God is Moving" with some help from Harvest Army's Choir in Bronx, New York.

MORE (SAYS THE LORD)

I want more of you
Give me more of You
I want more of you
Says the Lord

I'm not satisfied
Make Me all you desire
I want more of you
Says the Lord

Jesus is asking me, and He is asking you
What a privilege it is to give God more

I want all your thoughts
I want all your heart
I want all your words
Says the Lord (More, the Lord asks for more)

CHAPTER 9

More

The Story behind the Song

It's not all the time that we a hear song encouraging us to give more to God. It's normally the other way around. We are the ones who are used to asking God for more of Himself. So these days when we see a song title called "more" or "more of you" we tend to immediately assume the direction of us wanting more of a God who is All-powerful, All-knowing, Who changes not. But in this particular song, it is the Lord, the Sovereign King of the universe who is asking mere mortals for more. He is not really saying He requires more of us as in numbers or quantity, but He wants more of us, as in quality.

The Lord can use one person to shake a nation if that one individual is completely sold out to the Will of The Lord.

Remember Jonah?

Remember David?

And the list goes on. For God to impact the earth in the way He desires, He is seeking out a man, a vessel, an instrument, to wield in His hand. And it's not that He can't do it by Himself, but God is a God of order, divine order, and this order has established certain laws where this earth is concerned. Yes, He can come down and eradicate all evil, He can. He could have completely destroyed the spirits that had possessed the man in St. Mark 5, but Christ came to earth to restore man to his rightful position—where our God-given authority and rulership which was taken from us when Adam sinned, would be given humanity. Like kings over kingdoms, we would exercise His power and authority over the earth. But there is a problem; we live in the 21st century. The post-industrial era where we basically have time only to focus on meeting our three basic human needs: food, shelter and clothing.

Though many have exaggerated these requirements, like wanting to have too much of either of the three or all, it still falls in one of the above.

To some of us, penciling in God into our daily plans appear an impossible task, even though it should be the other way around, where we seek God to find out what His plans are, and work on being a part of it. We have all become so "busy" that we spend so little time with God, yet we give the boss most of our day, and by the time we get home to give God what He has asked, we fall asleep at the bedside five minutes into our prayer time.

Sometimes we don't even get to give God any of our time throughout the whole 24 hours we have in each day. Yes, 24 hours, but God gets not even one minute with us where we are settled enough to hear His voice. If I was In God's place, I would be hurt. For if I expected my daughter or son whom I love to come to me and spend time with me, yet after waiting for days, weeks, even years, all I get is "drive-by" hello or a ritualistic, religious sentiment, it would be disheartening.

If you don't understand what I mean by" drive-by" prayers, Its when for example, we just utter a very quick "thank you Lord for a new day" kind of thing to God, without even pausing to have a real conversation with the One who created us and knows our very makeup. When things like this happen, over time the enemy gradually erodes our connections to the Lord, and before we even know it, we either find ourselves compromising in areas we never imagined we would, or worst case scenario, we fall from grace.

The Lord is asking for more of you, and more of me. And we have to respond in earnest, for if God is asking us for more; it only means that He has an intention behind His request. I don't want to ever keep my God waiting to release something in my life, and in the end discover that it was my lack of response that hindered it. God never does anything or says anything without reason. He always has a plan. That's one of the reasons why I love Him so much. He is intentional, He is God.

Let's stop, and take an inventory of our lives, to see if we have become too full of other things other than the things of God. Let's pause right now to check ourselves to see if we have been responsive to the gentle voice of the Holy Spirit. At the end of this, all I want to hear is well done my good and faithful servant. I also don't want to just barely make it into heaven, I want to be so "maxed out" by the time I 'm ready to leave this earth as a result of my responsiveness to His voice and instructions.

I remember when I got this song, I was on a two month North American tour, and I was in St. Louis Missouri by this time. I was among the church family of Agape Time Ministries headed by Pastors John and Pam Dillon. The young people of this assembly were so on fire for God. Yes they were young, and yes most of them were not incredibly wealthy. Some of them had a history they weren't proud to discuss. But what struck me was that they were after one thing, and by all means, I must say the one thing that really matters.

They were hungry for God.

They did not just sit there prodding God to give them more of Himself, they were in active pursuit, and gave the Lord time to do His work in them. Worship sessions went as long as two to three hours sometimes. When they worshipped, they were not putting on a show to receive credit from man, they were really locked into God emptying themselves of what was, so God would fill them with Himself.

It does not matter how different your lifestyle is from mine, we all can give God more. We all can give God all of our heart; we all can give God more of the things we say by saying only what He wants us to say. We can give God more of our thoughts by maintaining a worshipful atmosphere at all times, by keeping our minds on Him.

We all can give God more, by always being open to the voice of His Spirit at all times. No matter where God is asking us to give Him more of, we can do it with His strength. And to many of us, as I said earlier, it may look impossible, but remember God will never ask us to do something without staying with us to help. Many of us have no idea how much our lives will change by our response. Well, I'm curious, I am eager to see what God will do when I respond to His beckoning.

The days are getting shorter; we are running out of time. Don't waste any more of it running from God, Let go, surrender to Him wanting more of you.

Psalms 51:17 says the sacrifices of God are a broken spirit, a broken and a contrite heart, He will not despise. This is the King of all kings singing to us. If He says he wants more, it's not a vain request, He has a motive. He wants to do more in your life, but He can't work with the little space you give Him. Give Him More! We sometimes think that giving God all our attention is a burden, rather than a privilege, or a blessing. Let's change our perspective as of now.

Lord our ears are open, our hearts are surrendered to You, we say yes.

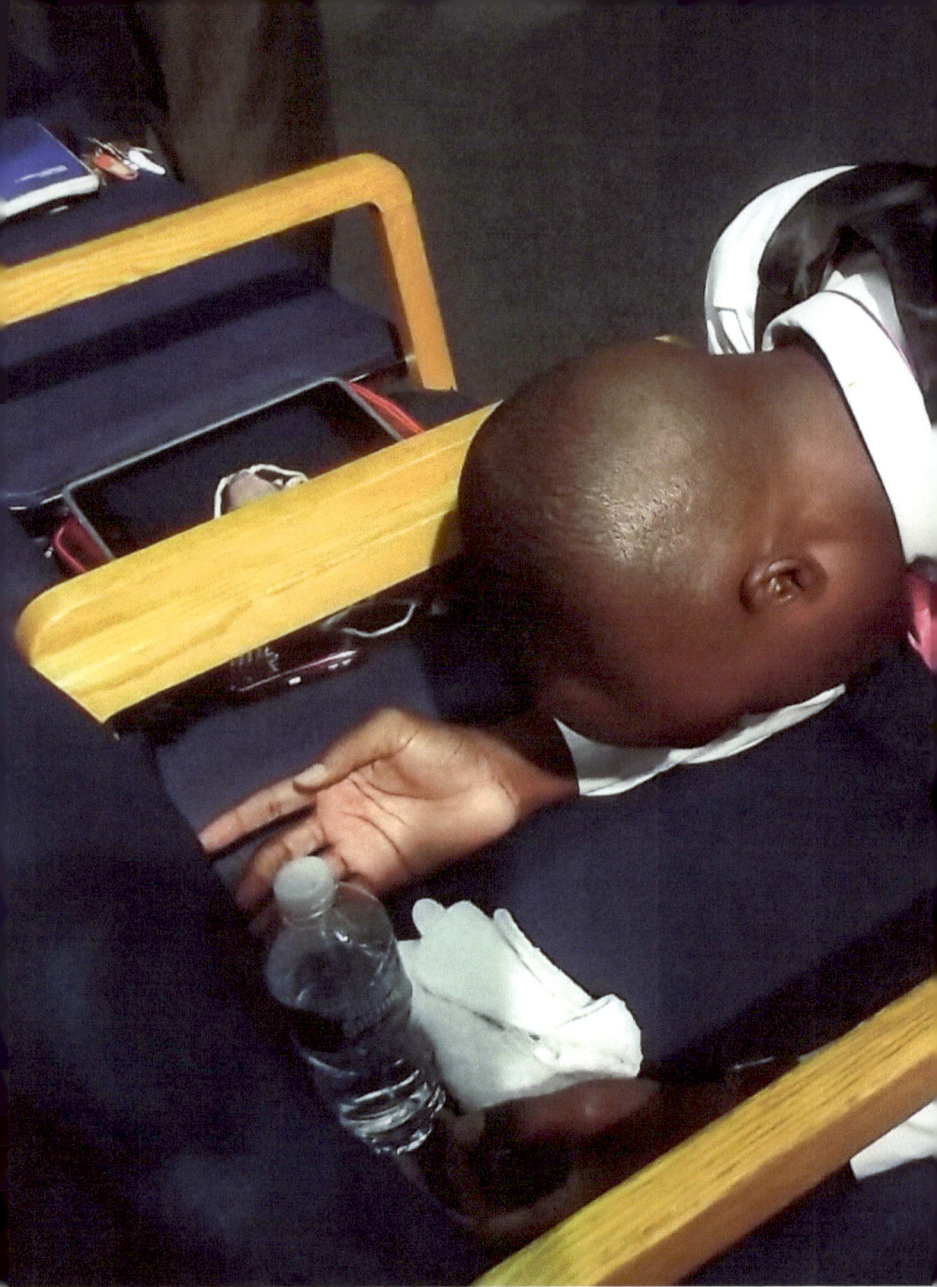

(ABOVE) Downswell always prays and seeks God's will before going on stage. He knows he needs "More" of God.

(OPPOSITE) Downswell delivering "More" on stage in Kingston.

YOU ARE LORD!

1.
I bow my life before You, and I worship at Your feet
I break my alabaster box, in worship unto Thee
I have been forgiven, I've been set free
No one else could have done, what You've done for me

> Chorus
> You are Lord, You are God
> You are Lord, You are God
> Adonai, You are God
> God and God alone, oh You are God

2.
You took me from the lowest, to live among kings
Your word stands forever, I receive Your promises
From the rising of the sun, until it's going down
You're name is worthy, God and God alone

Bridge
Holy, Holy, Holy
You are God Almighty
The earth is full, the earth is full
With Your glory

CHAPTER 10

You Are Lord!

The Story Behind the Song

This song speaks for itself. There is no God but our God.

So we declare throughout the whole earth, to every nation, region, territory, that the kingdoms of this world are become the kingdom of our Lord, and of His Christ, and He shall reign forever and ever (Revelations 11:15).

God is God, and there is none like Him. His word stands, when our opinion is voiced, acted upon, and faded away. He is holy, separate and above all. He chooses who He exalts, and who He brings down.We live in a world where many believe there is no absolute truth, but whether we believe or not, that does not affect God's self-esteem or image. He needs no one to defend Him; He is God all by Himself. He is my God.

Hanna was laughed at by Penninah, because she was not able to conceive, and in those times, it was tradition for a woman who was barren to be ostracized and rejected by her community. But Hanna knew that only God could help her. She had a pressing situation, and she was not about to give up because she hoped in God

It's no news that God can do what is impossible. But we must know and believe that He can really do it. And without faith, it is impossible to please God. "For he that cometh to God, must believe that He is, and that He is a rewarder to them that diligently seek Him" (Hebrews 11:6).

God came through for Hanna, and her opposition was confounded. "and they shall know that I am the Lord Your God" (Exodus 29:46).

How can we cut down a tree, furnish it into an image, and call it our God? And even though, some of us may scoff at that, whether we believe it or not, we may unknowingly place our jobs or our earthly possessions ahead of God.

Let us be careful to exalt God for who He is. He is and will always be. "The fear of the Lord is the beginning of wisdom" (Proverbs 9:10).

Let God be your everything.

Let your heart be His always.

Let Him guide you and direct your path. You will not falter, for He will hold you up. He will keep you.

God and God alone, He is God. "And you shall love the Lord your God, with all your heart, with all your soul, and with all your might" (Deut. 6:4, 5). We shall recognize that **You are Lord**.

(ABOVE) Downswell ministering in St. Louis Missouri at the annual Stir Up the Gifts Summit.

(LEFT) Downswell (CENTRE) between lead guitarist Jovan Norman and bassist Karl Gibson, ministering at the Nyammins and Jammins Festival in Montego Bay.

IF IT HAD NOT BEEN (Featuring Miriam Levy, Downswell's mother)

Chorus
If it had, not, been for the Lord, on my side
Where would I be? Where would I be?
If it had not been for the Lord on my side
Where would I be? Where would I be?

1.
He kept my enemies away
He let the sun shine through a cloudy day
Oh, He wrapped me in the cradle of His arms
When He knew I've been battered and torn,
So...

Chorus
If it had, not, been for the Lord, on my side
Where would I be? Where would I be?
If it had not been for the Lord on my side
Where would I be? Where would I be?

2.
He never left me all alone
He gave me peace and joy I've never known
He answered when I knelt to Him in prayer
And In victory the Lord showed me the way,
So...

Chorus
If it had, not, been for the Lord, on my side
Where would I be? Where would I be?
If it had not been for the Lord on my side
Where would I be? Where would I be?

CHAPTER 11

If It Had Not Been

The Story Behind the Song

There's one thing I'd like to begin by saying, and it's thank God for my mother, thank God for those single parents out there who give their all to their children's well-being. I call you unsung heroes, for if it had not been for you holding unto God's unchanging hand, where would some of us be?

I don't know where I would have been, had it not been for God who kept my mom going. All those hungry days when I was a child growing up, where she just did not have it, Yet she didn't compromise in her commitment to serving and trusting God.

God bless you mom. When you could not see his plan, when the path became foggy, you knew He would not allow His word over you to fail. Thank you for teaching me how to trust in God, even when everything and everyone around said not to.

I might not have had all the necessities during my childhood days, but she taught me to be grateful. I thank God for you. Now, the priceless investment you've made into my life, I cherish deeply, and promise to honour it.

If you are familiar with some of my past radio and television interviews, you might hear me talk a lot about my mom and wondered what happened to my father, just like what some may be doing right now. My dad is alive and well, and I love him very much. But let me tell you a story.

I remember when I was about 18 or 19 years old, the time when I really became curious and started asking my mother lots of questions. Questions like why did it seem as if my dad didn't care? Or has he called to check on me? Hence, one day, with her approval, I went on a journey. I drove about 300km from Kingston to Westmoreland, where he lived just to have a "talk".

If you're a male reading this, you know why I said it like that, because when it comes to talking, men can be very absent in that area. From very brief answers to "ask your mom" responses, we got it like that. So, you know I had to dig deep to access even the simplest of answers from my father. But I asked him this one important question that brought a change.

I called him by his name, because I was not used to calling him dad.

I asked, "Why does it seem as if you don't care about me? Why weren't you there?" He sighed, stared into space, dropped his head, and mumbled, "Son, I wanted to be there." This was breakthrough on so many levels, but he continued:

"I didn't have the money to take care of you."

I later discovered that my father was so proud of me he would tell the whole community how well his son was doing, but that's the problem, he told everyone else but me.

If it hadn't been for God who was in charge of my life, I would have been scarred and empty, so void of a father's approval and of his blessings. God brought men of influence into my life that guided me and did what my mom just could not physically do. God also ensured that I didn't grow bitter or angry at my father. I want to use my experience to encourage the fathers who are reading this book to do one thing...

Stay.

Even when you have nothing to give but your time.

Stay.

Even if you think that having that child was a big mistake.

Still stay.

God is a generational God, and the dysfunctional repetitions that have occurred in your family line can be broken today, if you step up, and be the one to break this cycle.

Will you be the one to cause a new day to dawn in your family?

When I minister to men behind bars today, the startling statistic is that about 80% of them never had a father who was there, to show them how to be a man. They never had a father to show them how to treat a lady right, and hence, all these men could do was to regurgitate only what they know or what the gangs taught being a man was. We have gangs raising children, because parents neglected and abandon them.

We have a generation coming up now who are desperately in need of help. We can hear them crying out "dad, where are you?" Step up fathers; we can cause the shift now.

To those fathers who stayed, amidst all heartache and struggles, I salute you.

Your reward is great. You remind us that there is actually hope. We thank God for you and we encourage you to stand. For those men who say that you don't know how or where to start, begin with committing your life over to God. For just like you, I had no clue of how to really be a man, a good husband, a great friend. But when I enrolled into the classroom of the Holy Spirit, everything began to change.

The process might not be easy, but it's possible. It will require grit and sheer determination, sacrifice and selflessness, but remember, with God, all things are possible.

Today I realize that because my father was not taught how to be the father he wanted to be, he didn't know how and or where to start. He had no one to guide him or to take the time to walk him through, so he did only what he knew. This cycle could have continued, but thanks be to God, who said enough is enough. Now, the old has passed, and the new is come. Today, my father is becoming a better man, learning each and every day. Our friendship is growing, and I pray for him every day that he would be saved.

Fathers, someone is asking you to stay. Someone is asking for you to come back home. No amount of money can compare to you just being there. No amount of material gift can compare to your small affirmations, "that was good son, I am proud of you my daughter."

Be the best you could ever be to your children, and even if your children seem to not appreciate your efforts, keep going, for God is watching. Keep on praying, keep on loving them, and remember when money is not there, you be there just the same.

(ABOVE) Downswell with his mother Miriam delivering a sensational song to a massive audience at Fun in the Son Festival.

There is one thing that is consistent across most of Downswell's ministry—he knows who to direct the attention to. Here he is with an audience in St. Ann, Jamaica, as they lift their hands to God in complete surrender.

WHEN I REMEMBER

1.

Feeling, dismayed by people who came and didn't stay,
They just walked away,
Heartbroken so many times but my friends keep telling me to try,
But doors have closed, I've been let down

> Chorus
> But when I remember, when I remember
> What You've done for me (Repeat)
> My hands went up, my hands went up,
> My praises broke free

2.

Shining through this darkness, is a light of Christ calling me to hope again,
It's not the end, God is a faithful friend
Bitterness wants to get the best of me, but I've missed the peace that
  comes through trusting in Thee,
Can I smile again?
Lord please hold my hand

Bridge
In my distress, I cried to the Lord, and He heard me, and delivered me
Some trust in chariots, some trust in horses but I will remember,
  the name of the Lord my God

CHAPTER 12

When I Remember

Behind the Song

This song is also very special to me. The Lord brought it to me when I was just about to wrap up writing the songs for the album, but I felt that there was one more song in this particular genre that I wanted to add to the album.

One fateful night, my wife and I were at home having a conversation in the kitchen and suddenly, I just heard the words in my spirit, "when I remember". I immediately ran to the living room and began to write. I somehow knew that this was the song I'd been waiting for all this time.

The chorus and the first verse came right away, but the second verse never came until the next day when I was sitting in my former lead guitarist's home waiting for him to get ready, for we had a studio session that day. The process to acquire the "bridge" of the song was quite interesting. I literally wrote about nine versions of the bridge before I came to a decision of which one I wanted to use.

I believe that one of the worst things that could ever happen to someone is when they not just forget their past, but forget what God has done for them. For often times, it's the experiences of the past that drives you into the future. I also believe that it's the enemy's intention to cause us to have amnesia regarding the work that God has wrought in our lives.

So when certain situations arise that seem way beyond us, all we need to do is look back and remember how God came through for us. Someone reading this might be dealing with the results of a tough divorce. It could be a job that you had intentions of going all the way to the top, but you suddenly got redundant. What do you do? These things can really affect us, and can either drive us from God or to Him. In situations like these, God speaks through this song to remind us it's not the end, that God is a faithful friend.

God sometimes carefully plans who comes into our lives, and who stays. Though it hurts sometimes when people leave, or when things don't work out the way we desire, we must not doubt that God can work it out. As hard as it seems, He does not make mistakes.

In the Book of Joshua 24, when the children of Israel were about to enter Canaan, Joshua encouraged them to recall or remember all God had done for them. This might have been because they were stepping into a greater place, and needed to keep in mind that it was God that brought this great change. Maybe it's because they were about to enter the Promised Land, but though it was the Promised Land, it was filled with many enemies, and their defeat could have appeared possible but would not come without sacrifice. They had to be reminded of the breakthrough that God gave them in the past, so they'll be faithful to know that God can and will finish what He began. Someone once told me that giants are not really a sign that we have exited Egypt, but proof that we have entered our promised land.

(ABOVE) Downswell delivering "When I Remember". He knows from where God has taken him, and is unashamed to lift up the name of Jesus at every opportunity.

(BELOW) Bass guitarist Karl Gibson, Band Leader of On the Shout Band.

ALREADY DONE *(with Ryan Mark)*

1.

I see you wondering why me in the midst of your adversity
But if you dare trust in me, I will supply all you need
I will take you over, I will take you over
I will never leave, to you I will cleave
I am standing right there, in the midst of your fear
I will be your brother man, stay close to Me my son

> Chorus
> It's already done, it's already done
> The victory is won, it's already done
> I will not die here even though I've cried here
> The victory is won, it's already done

2.

I often wonder why me, why they took my family
And when the world is falling on my shoulders, yes I fall on my knees
Lord takes me over, please take me over
Please do not leave, to you I will cleave
I know that you're right here, standing in my tears
You are my Father, close to me Master

> Chorus
> It's already done, it's already done
> If You said it's done, then it's already done
> I will not die here, even though I've cried here
> The victory is won, cause You said its won

Bridge
I'm running I'm running I'm running
But sometimes I don't feel like running
Keep pressing, keep pressing
Though sometimes you don't feel like pressing
Keep your eyes on Me, will you trust in Me
I will be with you to the end

CHAPTER 13

Already Done

The Story Behind the Song

Thanks to Minister Ryan Mark for doing this song with me.

When God says He makes known the end from the beginning, it reminds me of an architect who draws up a plan or blue print of what the finished product is even before laying the first block. People pass by the property and see nothing, but the architect knows, it's already complete. See, whatever God began in you is already complete. Every resource, everything needed to finish is in place. So though some may say to you "what are you doing?" Or "I don't see anything?" Keep building, keep moving forward, for you and God (the architect) know what exists in the unseen, which shortly will manifest (become visible). Do not get weary or deceived by the visible, for greater things are happening in the unseen. That's why we walk by faith and not by sight."For I AM your God, and there is no other" (Isaiah 46:9-10).

The Lord said to Jeremiah," Before I formed you in the womb I knew [and] approved of you [as my chosen instrument], and before you were born I separated and set you apart, consecrating you; [and] I appointed you as a prophet to the nations" (Jeremiah 1:5 AMP).

For those whom He foreknew (of whom He was aware and loved beforehand), He also destined from the beginning [foreordaining them] to be molded into the image of His Son (and share inwardly His likeness), that He might become the firstborn among many brethren. And those whom He thus foreordained, He also called; and those whom He called, He also justified (acquitted, made righteous, putting them into right standing with Himself). And those whom He justified, He also glorified [raising them to a heavenly dignity and condition or state of being]. Romans 8:29-30 (AMP).

God, in His omniscience, saw your birth before you were born. Not just that, but He looked ahead and saw the battles and wars you would fight, but you might have had no chance of victory if it wasn't for the cross of Calvary. Through this image which once signified shame, you and I have been redeemed, and given a new lease on life. A fresh chance to make every day count for the Glory of God, but not just that, for when Christ died on the cross, He said "It is finished" which heralded across the whole universe the message of victory. Victory for you, victory for me.... And we can look forward to the future knowing that every battle we fight, Christ has already conquered for us, it refreshes our faith. You may cry, but you're in Him and His life in you will give you all you need to last.

Fight this good fight of faith, for faith is not believing that God will do it, but it is knowing that He has already done it. You shall not die, but live to declare the works of the Lord. (Psalms 118:17).

In performance of "It's Already Done" with Ryan Mark, with whom he collaborates on this song.

Kevin shares the stage with fellow gospel artiste Pastor Ryan Mark Reynolds as they deliver "It's Already Done".

(ABOVE) Making these kinds of visits is always a part of Downswell's schedule, no matter how busy he is. Here he meets students of St. Benedict's Primary in Harbour View, Kingston .

(OPPOSITE TOP) Downswell's band as they deliver "It's already Done" from left: Dale Lowe, Wendell Lawrence, Adrian Scarlett and Jovan Norman with Karl Gibson not in the shot.

(OOPOSITE BOTTOM) Downswell on stage at a Youth Symposium in downtown Kingston.

I NEED YOU

1.
Even if the earth a quake 9.0 pon di rich, the Richter scale
Whether inna (in) prison or inna jail, bars of steals will fail
Mi ago (I will) find every way to get to you cause only you and you alone will do
I don't wanna hear about no other one, Lord I'm nothing without you

2. *There's a relentless generation that keeps pressing in*
We're not comfortable we just want more of Him
Willing to let go of every single form of sin
Lord come in (Lord Jesus)
I realize for me to tell another man about you, I got to know you
I realize for me to show another man who you are, I can't stay far

Bridge
Jesus i need you, more than the next heart beat
I need you—more than I need me
I need you—more than the air i breathe, Lord it's your faced I seek,
I need all of thee
For with you—I'm gonna ride through the storm
But without you—I'll be all alone
You're love is more than life to Me, Lord open our eyes to see

Chorus
That we need you, no matter what a gwaan (going on)
A you calm the storms in my life
I need you,
I'll climb the highest mountains; I'll swim the deepest seas cause Lord
It's got to be you
Every single day mi pray, I wanna know something new about you today,
I need you, I need you, I need you

CHAPTER 14

I Need You

The Story Behind the Song

I love this song. It was written when I was on a North American/Caribbean tour in 2010. I was in Florida to be specific. Interestingly, the following year, a 9.0 magnitude earthquake devastated Japan. I found it interesting that when I decided to put this size magnitude of an earthquake in the first verse of this song, it was placed there as a maximum, and a figure I never thought would really be materialized, since I was speaking metaphorically to symbolized extremes, and that nothing can keep me from God.

This song speaks for itself, I need the Lord, and no matter how much I accomplish in life, I will still need to fill that part of me that nothing or no one else can fill. No matter how many people say they are there for me, there is no better bosom to rest my weary head on. Inasmuch as I appreciate their presence; there is just no better presence than the Lord.

Lord, we need You.

A very moving moment with keyboardist Dale Lowe.

The audience looks on as Minister Downswell delivers "I Need You" at Denbigh Show in Clarendon.

Downswell's three background vocalists as they minister.

SITUATIONS

Chorus
I see the people them a suffer
And I see the people them a bawl
But I see my people getting tougher
On Jesus Christ them learning how to call

I see situations getting rougher
My brother man yuh (your) back's against the wall
But I see my people getting stronger
On Jesus Christ them learning how to call

1.
I don't know about you, but this is the truth
When Jesus Christ rose, all hell was rebuked
Right now I stand here a freed young man
Holiness and obedience are my only intention
I know the battle is really not mine
But all that I do is stand on Christ
Every trial that I see in front of me
Are already won by Jesus Christ on Calvary

2.
Mi (my) brother when you a go through, Him seh (said) Him naah (not) go leave
Mama mi know you son a bad but don't come off your knees
Sister girl, I feel your pain, tears a fall like rain, listen what I'm saying
God has much more for you, He said He loves, He won't reject you, come as you are
Grace is amazing, it's your invitation, I say it again, come as you are

Bridge
He's the king of Kings, He can do any thing
If you just call on Him, some way you must win
Say glory, Hallelujah, Jesus, I need you

CHAPTER 15

Situations

The Story Behind the Song

The word of God states that whoever calls on the name of the Lord shall be saved (Acts 2:21).

It did not say if you look a certain way or if you don't have this particular trait, then you can't come to God. Whosoever will, may come. Come unto Me, all ye that labour and are heavy-laden and I will give you rest. Take my yoke upon you, and learn of me; for I am meek and lowly in heart: and ye shall find rest unto your souls. My yoke is easy, and my burden is light (St Matthew 11:28-30). But as many as received him, to them gave He the power to become the sons of God, [even] to them that believe on his name (St John 1:12).

Let's face the music; we cannot make it without Jesus.

And even if we think we have it all together, the Bible also says that "For when they shall say, Peace and safety; then sudden destruction cometh upon them, as travail upon a woman with child; and they shall not escape" (1 Thessalonians 5:3).

Everybody has tough times these days, but I cannot tell you one instance where I made it through without God. I cannot make it without Christ, His name alone is my identity, and resounds throughout my whole being.

This song is about directing people to Christ. I share what God has done for me, and how He can do the very same for the one who does not know Him. It introduces varying situations that people are facing, and how God can change it all if we learn to call on Him. More and more people are turning to God every day, and for some it's because they have tried everything, and had run out of options. It's an invitation to those who might spend the next 5-10 years still trying other things to not waste all this valuable time, and to just call on Jesus right now.

Experience is the best teacher, so I speak from my experience to try and prevent others from going down the same path. I broke out in tears while recording this song, something you might just hear somewhere in the Bridge. That's how passionate I was in delivering this song. Men and women are dying and going to hell every single day. It hurts to know that if they had only known Christ, their destination would have been different. I held nothing back in this song. People need to know that Jesus has not forsaken them, He is waiting in anticipation to hear their call, so He may run to them.

We must know that Jesus is everything and more. No matter our situation, Jesus can make us better. He will bring change to what we deem as unchangeable. He can repair the irreparable. Each and every man has his own situation, but it is God who makes all the difference. Being a Christian, does not immunize us from troubles, but when we surrender our lives to God, we now have the divine ability to conquer our adversities.

God makes all the difference.

If you are reading this and feel convinced that you are ready to surrender your life to God, then pray this prayer with me:

> Lord Jesus, I believe that You are the Son of God. I believe that You died for me, but You rose on the third day, I believe that You are God, and I surrender my life to You right now. Change my heart, and teach me how to serve You. You are my Saviour, my redeemer, and now the centre of my life. In Jesus' name. Amen.

You are now a child of God.

The Holy Spirit now has access; your life will never be the same again. Find a Bible, one you are able to understand, find a church that stands on the undiluted word of God and preaches Jesus Christ, the saviour of mankind. Build friendships with people who will challenge you to get closer to God, and live each day like it's your last.

Welcome my friend into the Kingdom of God.

WHEN WE WORSHIP

Hear the mountains falling; Hear shackles them fall
It's the worshippers rising; To the clarion call (Repeat)

> Chorus
> When we worship—Come before You with a joyful heart
> When we worship—Here in Your Holy presence Lord do Your part
> When we worship—It's all about You from the very start
> When we worship—When we worship
> When we worship—Watch the enemy's kingdom fall
> When we worship—God a go crumble all Your Jericho wall
> When we worship—Watch Your faith grow strong and tall

1.
I am a worshipper I ain't scared
I am a worshipper I ain't afraid
Many things going on
From dusk until dawn
But when we worship the battle is already won
Come higher with me let's go deeper
Go a look for the worshipper sister and the worshipper brother
Walk out without a doubt
Cause your worship is a weapon that will drive every demon out, out, out, come out!

2.
Tears are a language that God understands
But He's seeking true worship to release His power on this land
The enemy plan fi shut your mouth and bind your hand
But where there is true worship there His kingdom will surely come
Many say they're not worthy, cause they've messed up big time
But where I've been if I tell you, it might blow your mind
When we choose to worship in the midst of crisis
Jehovah Shalom will be there my brother don't quit, don't quit, don't quit

Vamp
Hear the mountains falling; Hear the shacke them fall
It's the worshippers rising; To the clarion call

CHAPTER 16

When We Worship
The Story Behind the Song

This song is a call; it's a beckoning, for the true worshippers to be seen, to arise, and to not be afraid. It depicts a dramatic scene where an army, God's army, responds to the blowing of a trumpet, which is God calling us to attention.

As a worshipper, we often go through challenges, but we don't look at things the way others do. We find every reason to give God glory. We are not oblivious to reality, but we know Who controls it. If we do not look at it the way Christ sees it, the intensity of situations can end up stealing our joy, our peace and our praise. Over time, we find ourselves being pushed into a place of compromise.

In the Bible, the sounding of a trumpet would signal different things, but this sound is one which jolts us to attentiveness, purposefulness, focus, and for us to know who we are and to Whom we belong. Today, people are so confused, we have got to be the lamp positioned just right so others can see this light, the light of Christ in us. "We are the light of the world, a city on a hill that cannot be hidden" (St. Matthew 5:14).

I had an event in New York once, and a couple of people were standing at the entrance of the venue talking about the law that was passed where church sessions were no longer allowed to be held in schools. So many churches had to either shut down or relocate.

Well in the midst of this panicky conversation, I jumped in and said, in situations like this where laws like these are being passed, and people are becoming increasing fearful, it's the perfect time for the true servant of God to step in and establish peace.

We should not be alarmed by these things, for we serve a God who orchestrates world events, so we need to use these opportunities to display the true character of Christ.

This worship is not just verbal worship; it's us displaying all the image of Christ in these tough times. Whether we believe it or not, someone is watching us, it's a challenge to be honest, when everyone else is being dishonest. It's a challenge to be true, when others seem to compromise the truth of God's word. It's a challenge to stand, when everyone else seems to be falling. God is counting on us to change the world we live in.

When the world sees God in us, they will marvel, they will become curious, and start to pursue this thing that causes you to be the way you are, creating the perfect opportunity to introduce Jesus Christ to them.

When we worship the King of kings, things happen that our limited sphere of operation can't decipher. When we worship, we introduce the realm of the supernatural into our natural world. We introduce the God who is unchanging into a world that constantly changes.

The world is waiting to see more, and if we truly practice the presence of God, there's no telling what God can do. God can do what He says He will, but it's our responsibility to bring His presence where we are, to invite Him in, so He can display and do what no man can. And when men see God's goodness, they will worship Him as God.

Where are the soldiers who march at the cadence of heavens beat?

Come to attention, stand in your place, be who you are, the world is waiting.

For when we worship, watch the enemy's kingdom fall, God will cause our Jericho walls to crumble. But we worship God only for who He is, not for what we want Him to do.

"When We Worship", God's presence shows up, and does more than we could imagine.

Downswell and his team delivers "When We Worship," at Jamaica College in Kingston, Jamaica.

Acknowledgements

I extend thanks to my wife, Marsha, for being my greatest inspiration behind this book; for loving and challenging me to keep on studying and reading, no matter how much I thought I already knew.

Thanks to my mother Miriam, who never fails to inspire me with her tenacity and unconditional love.

Thanks to Wendell Lawrence and the Spurr Music Empire team for their hard work behind the scenes. Thanks to the intercessors and my mentors Dr. Henley Morgan, Pastors John and Pam Dillon, Mother Reynolds, Pastor Hamilton, Pastor Michael Rose, Bishop T.D. Jakes, Dr. Myles Munroe and others who, whether directly and indirectly, have provided a compass and light on this path to impacting, influencing and changing lives for the honour and glory of God.

Thanks to my team who stuck with me from the beginning until now. Thanks to all my supporters who stop by now and then whether through social media or at events, in the supermarket or at the stop light to leave an encouraging word.

About the Author

Kevin Downswell is an International Gospel Recording Artiste. Kevin's gift surfaced at about the age of 13 years. Family members knew he was different as he stood out amongst his peers. From a young age, he was always passionate in all his pursuits. Amidst the trying times he experienced during his childhood years, he always found a way to rise above his limitations.

Downswell could have easily succumbed to the many sources of pressure and struggles which he faced. However, with patient tenacity and with God by his side, he not just survived, but came out a better man. Ordained to the office of an Evangelist in 2005, the same year he graduated from University (U.W.I) with a Bachelors Degree in biochemistry, Downswell's aim was to become a medical doctor; however this all changed when God stepped in, leading him to become a full-time Minister of the Gospel.

This was not a very easy decision, he received wise counsel from many influential people, who were there to help guide him and see him through this transition. He knew God's unmistakable voice, for this was the same voice that gave him direction throughout his earlier years. Now, many years after making that life-changing decision, God has blessed him tremendously, bringing to pass that which is written in 1st Samuels 15 vs. 22: "Obedience is better than sacrifice...."

The Musical Journey

In 2003, the world was introduced to Kevin Downswell, when he won the Jamaica Cultural Development Commission's Gospel Competition with the entry song "Praise". He also received the award for "Most Outstanding Performer" in the same competition. In 2005, he had his first major hit song entitled, "Naah Bow" on which he collaborated with DJ Nicholas and Jermaine Edwards. This song won the 2006 Marlin Awards for Best Reggae Recording of the Year and has become an anthem to youths across the Caribbean. It did not end there however, as he was one of a few Jamaican artistes chosen to be a part of an international compilation album produced by Tennyson Walters of OFMB located in New Jersey, U.S.A. This Album went on to become the first Reggae Album to top the New York and Florida charts simultaneously in 2006.

Downswell's two contributions to this album, "Evildoers—Fret Not" and "Since the World Didn't Love Me" were now being heard around the world in various places, including but not limited to, U.S, Japan, Africa, Europe and the Caribbean. God was gradually enlarging his territory. During all these achievements and hard work, he was steadily working on his debut album, releasing singles and building his repertoire. In May 2006, Downswell went on his first international tour in Canada, which lasted for one month, and then returned home to accelerate the completion of his album.

The Debut Album "Close To You"

In May, 2008, "Close To You" the title of his debut album was officially launched in Kingston, Jamaica. This album contains fifteen tracks and steadily rose to become one of Jamaica's loved albums to date. The title track "Close To You", is currently one of the most popular worship songs in Jamaica and other places, and other popular songs from the album are namely: "Stand", "Shout", "Praise", "Nothing Just Happens", "I Can Feel Your Glory", "Change Is Coming", "Joy" and "In The Name of Jesus". These songs have been changing lives around the world in places such as Canada, the U.S, and Europe, the Caribbean, France and certain parts of Africa.

The album and some of the individual songs have won numerous awards such as The Marlin Awards (Caribbean Gospel Music Awards), The Atlanta Gospel Music Awards, EME award nomination, Paramount MEGA Gospel Music Awards among others. Many have testified how each song they have come to enjoy gave them enough faith to go through some very challenging times.

Amidst these accolades and achievements, however, Downswell remains focused and humble. His ultimate aim is to be a tool in the hand of the Lord, to be used to draw all men unto God. He has shared the stage with some of Gospel's greatest including, Donnie McClurkin, Kirk Franklyn, Byron Cage, Alvin Slaughter, John Hagee, Tye Tribbette, Marvin Winans, Myles Monroe, William McDowell, William Murphy, Paul S. Morton, Hezekiah Walker, Lecrae, Michael W. Smith, and many others.

The Sophomore Album

On June 1, 2012, Downswell released his highly anticipated sophomore album entitled, "The Search Continues". The album is a clear-cut world class production, and varies between reggae, alternative and ballads that tug at your heart. Four (4) singles, which were released to promote this album had already been nominated or have won numerous awards: "Forgiven", "That's Enough", "God is Moving" and "Already Done". The songs emerge from Downswell's rich and deep experience growing up in the inner city. He was always viewed by his peers to be one who loved God and has never been afraid to express it. The journey to move from his past challenges to where he is today is a priceless feat to which he attributes all honour to God. He is an inspiration to the youths of today and continually encourages them that they can do all things through Christ and be more than they've ever dreamed.

Kevin Downswell is happily married and has the heart of a worshipper.

Motto is St. John 3:30: "He must increase, I must decrease".